The Bighead

Rod Ellis and
Sarah Murray

Illustrated by Trish de Villiers

Good morning children, the teacher says. This is Majozi. He is a new boy.

Majozi is very big.
He looks strong.
He does not look very friendly.

It is break time.
The children are in the playground.

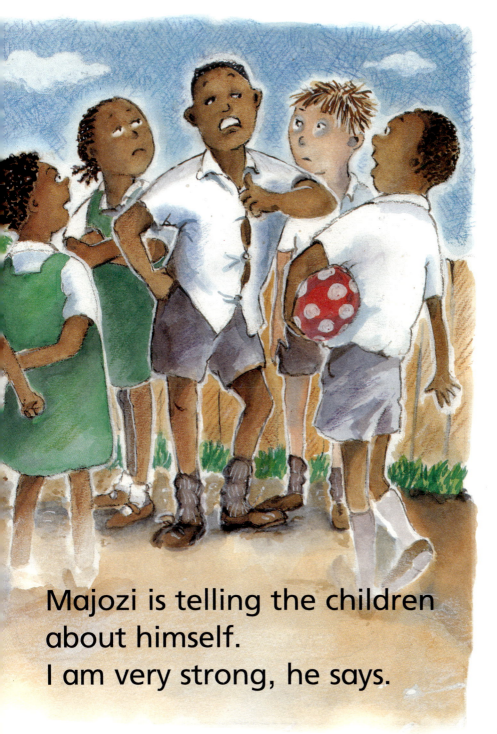

Majozi is telling the children about himself.
I am very strong, he says.

Can you run very fast? Majozi asks Luke.
No, Luke says.
I can, Majozi says. Look at me.

Majozi runs round the playground.
He is very fast.

Can you jump very high?
Majozi asks Lorato.
No, Lorato says.
I can, Majozi says. Look at me.

Majozi jumps over the fence.
It is very high.

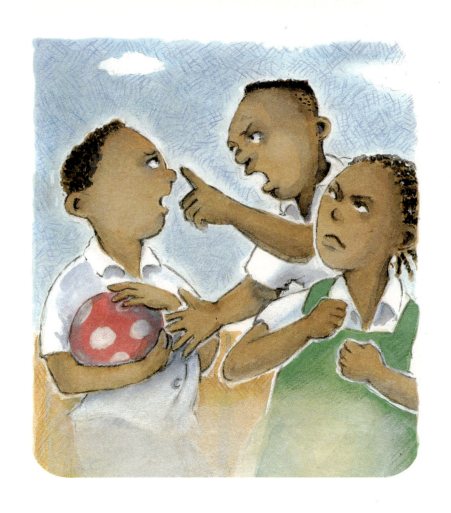

Can you kick a ball a very long way? Majozi asks Tommy.
No, Tommy says.
I can, Majozi says. Look at me.

Majozi kicks the ball.
It goes a very long way.

Phumela says to Majozi,
We can see you are big and strong. But can you do this?

She closes her left eye and keeps her right eye open.

Majozi tries.
He cannot do it.

The children laugh at Majozi.
Bighead, says Phumela.

Activity

Look at these three pictures. What is Majozi doing?

What is Majozi trying to do here?